CW00326704

PRUNING IN THE
FRUIT GARDEN

F. Hilkenbäumer

Edited by
A. M. Toms, NDA, M.I. Biol.

Illustrated by
Hans Preusse

BLANDFORD PRESS
POOLE   DORSET

Contents

Introduction

The art of pruning should have at its basis the establishment of balance between the vegetative and fruiting growth of an entire framework of a tree throughout its life, i.e. the young, mature, and older stages of a tree's development. Further, it is important to adjust this basic tree framework to fit in with natural available space. This is achieved by keeping a tree pruned in the proper manner.

The whole concept of pruning has undergone considerable changes in recent years. Previously, it was considered preferable to produce a sturdy framework to the tree at the expense of early cropping. Today, smaller trees are preferred. These fruit earlier, produce a high yield, are relatively simple and quick to prune, and during their natural fruiting lifetime make the best possible use of the ground space.

Just as important as the early yield of the young tree is to the overall crop, so is the maintenance of satisfactory, sturdy new growth to the whole fruiting life of the tree. This is achieved by careful inspection and pruning of the fruit wood. When the production of new vegetative growth starts to decrease, and the size and quality of the fruit crop deteriorates, one must reduce the size of the tree by hard pruning. This has to be done in order to renovate the tree. As far as tree fruit is concerned, varieties (cultivars) which are unsuitable can be replaced by grafting more desirable varieties on the old stock, provided conditions are suitable.

For this edition, all the results of our many recent trials and observations have been taken into consideration. These trials concerned the physiologically correct and practical pruning techniques of both pip and stone fruits. The fundamental principles of pruning are explained, since these modify the growth and produce the tree framework. They are also essential for an understanding of the pruning techniques that are described. The pruning of berry bushes and grapes in their various stages of development is also discussed.

In order to provide a better understanding of the pruning work required, the illustrations provide a step-by-step guide to the consecutive stages to be followed in pruning. Throughout the illustrations, those parts of the tree framework which are actually to be removed are shown in red.

The final result of the pruning operation is very largely dependant upon the other measures which are taken. An even balance between the young shoots of new growth and the produce of fruit trees or bushes, is easier to establish when the pruning is suitably adapted. This should match not only the strength of the selected variety and stock, but also the soil type and fertilisers to be used on the garden.

A reduction of growth can be obtained in pip fruit through the use of dwarf stocks, Malling IX and Quince, and through a higher grafting of the scions on the stocks. Stocks producing reduced growth in stone fruit have not yet been discovered.

As a complement to pruning and also as a way of counteracting unfavourable weather conditions, the development of both growth and fruit buds can be influenced further by fruit thinning, by supplying plant nutrients and by the use of growth regulators.

A concentrated, single 'dose' of nitrogen fertiliser, regular grass mulchings in the work lane, and use of herbicides to keep down the weeds in the tree rows, have all been shown to help the growth of young shoots. However, excessive young shoot development runs parallel with a deterioration in fruit quality, and so to some extent shoot growth inhibition has a considerable influence on fruit production. The required cut back in shoot growth can be obtained by a moderate application of nitrogen fertiliser. This should be applied in several small doses, and occasionally leaving the tree rows unweeded. A light pruning when carried out jointly with the correct dose of nitrogen fertiliser (and preferably not in the summer), can also reduce the infection of canker.

Obtaining the correct, open tree framework, with young shoot formation on the outside, lessens the risk of attack by the usual diseases.* Light frameworks are also important for good penetration and coverage by chemical sprays. This is important for a satisfactory control of pests such as aphids and red spider, and diseases such as *Gloeosporium*. The control of mildew can usually only be achieved by chemical methods and supplemented by the pruning of infected terminal buds of the young shoots.

Only when carried out in conjunction with other essential garden operations can pruning produce a satisfactory result.

The author would like to acknowledge the collaboration of Dr. Gustav Engel and thank him for his help as co-worker.

*See A. M. Toms and M. H. Dahl, *Pests and Diseases of Fruit and Vegetables in the Garden,* Blandford Press Ltd.

THE THEORY OF PRUNING

BASIC PRINCIPLES

Natural zones of vegetative growth and fruiting are indicated below.

Preferred Growth Zones   Preferred Fruiting Zones

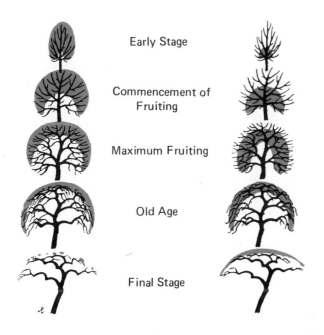

Early Stage

Commencement of Fruiting

Maximum Fruiting

Old Age

Final Stage

During the development of the tree framework, growth and fruiting zones will shift according to the particular period of the life of the tree.

5

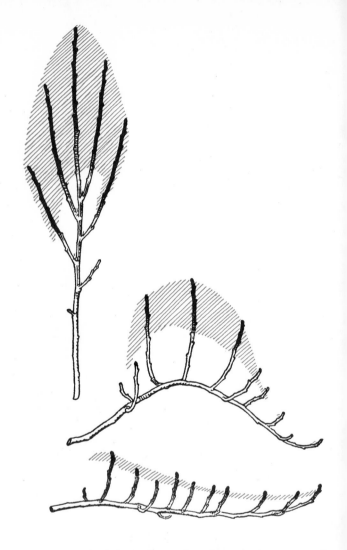

On the vertical branches, the tips produce growth, but on arched branches only the apex buds are growth-producing. On horizontal branches, all buds on the upper side are equal in size and shape.

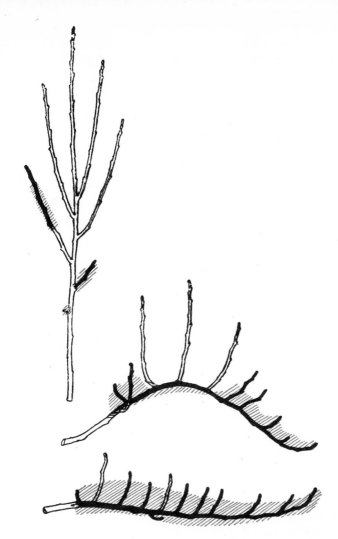

In general, weak shoots produce the fruit buds.
However, they can also be produced on strong shoots
of some varieties, provided the shoots are arranged in
a horizontal or sloping position within the tree's
framework.

7

The General Effect of Pruning on the Various Zones

Growth Zones

Incorrect growth of the lateral branches, which grow at a steep angle to the central axis, results in over-development of the top framework of the tree. This then causes lack of spreading and basal branches. With correct pruning, the leading branch will grow at a wider angle. The young shoot formation becomes currently adjusted on this new basis.

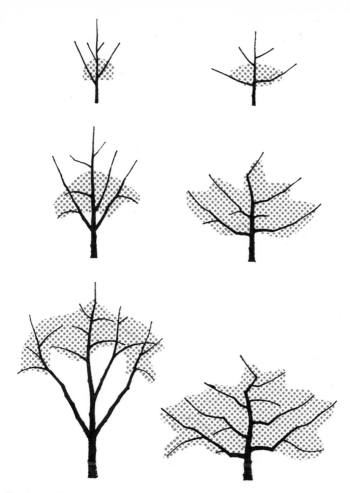

Fruiting Zones

Only by correct pruning can earlier fruiting be obtained, together with an increase in crops of early produce and regular fruiting on all parts of the tree framework. In contrast, the crop produced by the incorrectly trained framework, is way above ground level.

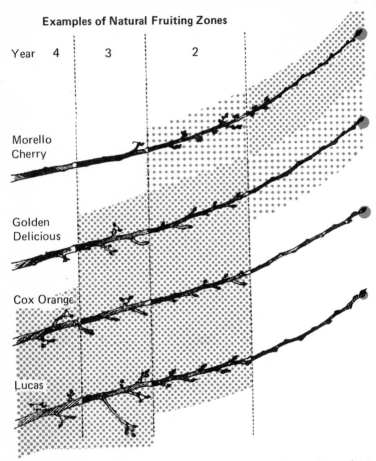

Examples of Natural Fruiting Zones

Year   4   3   2

Morello
Cherry

Golden
Delicious

Cox Orange

Lucas

Principal Flowering Zones on One-to-Four-Year-Old Wood

Morello Cherry and other stone fruits usually produce blossom on one-year-old wood. The prolific flowering Golden Delicious produces most blossom, but the shy-flowering Cox seldom has any blossom at all on one-year-old wood. Pear trees (e.g. Lucas) blossom in a similar manner to the Cox.

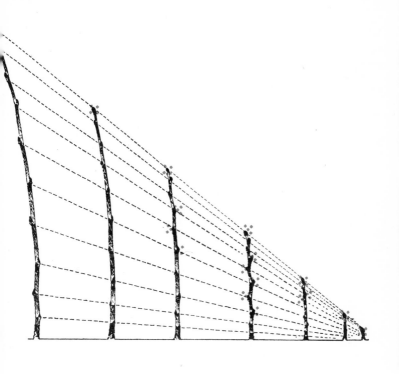

Blossom Formation on Pip Fruit Trees with Different
Shoot Lengths
Blossom formation commences on the terminal bud
and increases the shorter and more horizontally inclined is the shoot.

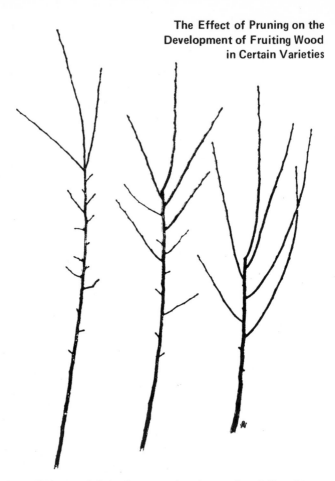

The Effect of Pruning on the Laterals of One-Year-Old Main Shoots

Without any pruning back of the main shoots, many short, flat side-shoots are produced and this speeds up the production of blossom. More severe pruning back produces a few stronger shoots, which grow more vertically and produce less and later blossoms.

12

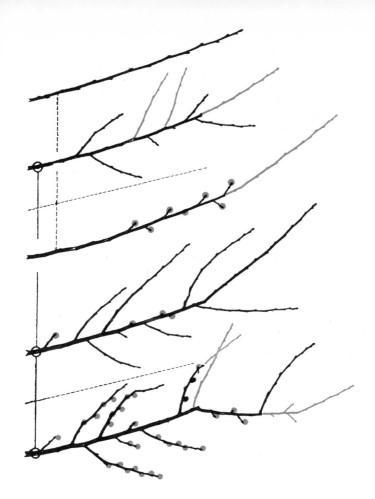

Modification Pruning to Fruiting Wood on Strong One-Year-Old Cox

With reasonably good growth, vigorous shoots on Cox either produce no blossom at all in the second year, or it falls off. By very careful pruning, i.e. leaving only the short, weak growth at the end of the second year, the fruiting wood for the third year can be established and this will produce increased blossom and fruit.

13

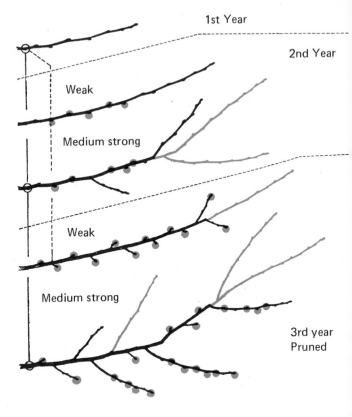

1st Year

2nd Year

Weak

Medium strong

Weak

Medium strong

3rd year
Pruned

Modification Pruning to Fruiting Wood of Weaker, Slanting Young Shoots of Cox

The weaker and more horizontally inclined young shoots in the second year already have plenty of flower buds, but not much growth. Diverting the shoots or a single pruning back above the upper flower buds on the second year growth prevents premature ageing of these fruiting branches.

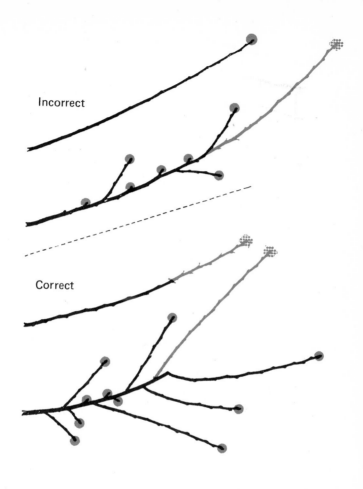

Incorrect

Correct

Correct Pruning for Fruiting on Strong One-Year-Old Shoots of Golden Delicious

With very prolific blooming varieties, heavy flowering and fruiting produces such large crops that fruit production is reduced in the following year. This is true even on strong one-year-old shoots.

15

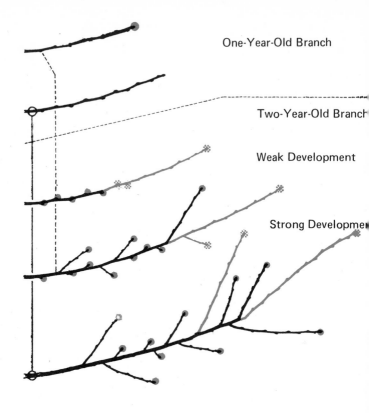

One-Year-Old Branch

Two-Year-Old Branch

Weak Development

Strong Development

Correct Pruning for Fruiting Wood Production on Weak to Medium-Strong Young Shoots of Golden Delicious

Weak, one-year-old shoots of Golden Delicious produce flowers only from terminal buds. Without pruning back, more vigorous blossom is not produced until the second year. Weak, two-year-old fruiting wood without new shoots must be shortened by about half. Somewhat stronger one-year-old fruiting branches must either be diverted to a lateral branch or not pruned at all.

16

PRUNING TECHNIQUES

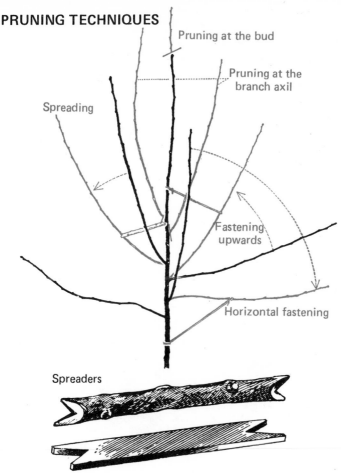

Pruning at the bud

Pruning at the branch axil

Spreading

Fastening upwards

Horizontal fastening

Spreaders

Spreading, Horizontal Fastening and Upright Fastening

In order to produce a balanced tree framework, shoots which are much too upright can be spread out or fastened back horizontally. Shoots which are too horizontal—particularly the relatively weaker shoots—can be fastened back in more upright positions.

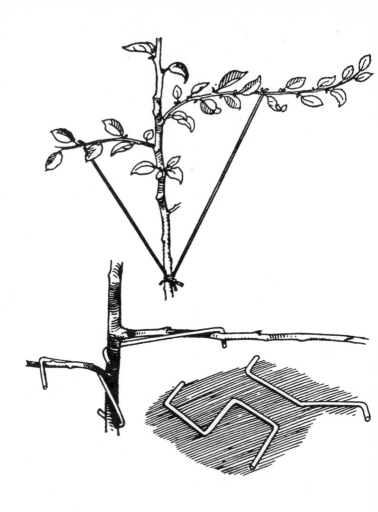

Instead of tying young shoots into a more horizontal position, fastening clamps can be used to advantage. This artificially shaped fruiting branch grows less vigorously but produces earlier and more abundant blossom than upright shoots.

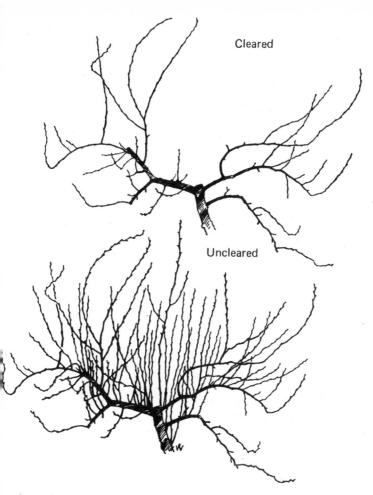

Cleared

Uncleared

Summer Clearance of Sprouts

All hard pruning, particularly a restriction of the branch framework, leads to the production of numerous soft shoots or sprouts. Most of these must be removed and the quickest and simplest way is to rip off the sprouting buds by hand. The scar left behind heals quickly and easily.

Here is part of a tree framework in the summer. There is sufficient foliage and little work is needed. Shoots which are not ripped out, later require time-wasting, individual pruning and the scars left after removal are delayed in healing. Thus, the growth of the required new shoot is curtailed.

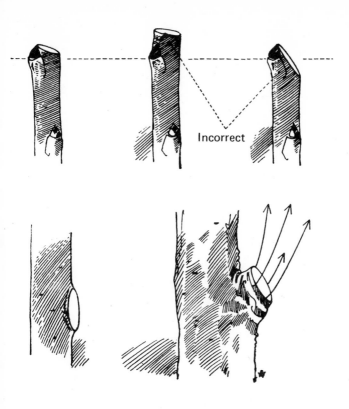

Incorrect

Pruning with Secateurs and Saw

Secateurs should be used in such a way that the lower wound cut is in line with the bud base. If the cut is too high, a dead stub is formed on the pruning wound, whilst if it is too low, the upper bud is easily dried out. A saw cut should be made at the same angle as the branch and flush to the remaining branch (lower left). This prevents the growth of numerous sprouts. Where the production of new shoots and branches is to be encouraged, a small stump is left to protect the buds at the base of the removed branch (lower right).

Use of Secateurs on Young Shoots

The secateurs must be used on the shoot from below as shown (left). Using even, light pulls on the shoot with the left hand, the work becomes easier and the result is neater. If the secateurs are used from above and downwards (right) the work is made more difficult, and the shoot tears easily at the pruning cut.

Sawing Technique on Larger Branches

In order to avoid splitting sawn branches, make one cut from below, nearly through to the middle of the branch at about 8 inches (20 cm) from the trunk. Then saw through from above. The cut is then made without splitting. Saw off the remainder of the stump from above so that the cut wound is flush with the trunk, and the scar will heal much easier.

23

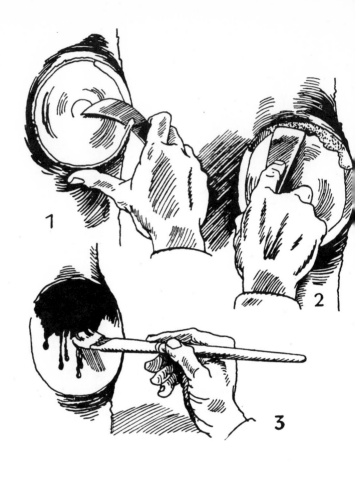

Treatment of Wounds

To encourage wound-healing, the edges of the cut surface should be smoothed with a sharp knife and treated with a tree wax, or preferably, a proprietary wound sealant containing a fungicide (to prevent any infection through the wound).

24

Pruning Aids

Fruiting can be promoted by interupting the flow of sap upwards through the tree by ring barking. Using a wire for marking the rings, a ½-inch (1.5 cm) wide strip of bark around the trunk is then carefully cut out in April–May. Root pruning, by cutting through the outside roots around the tree, also reduces the flow of plant nutrients and so encourages the production of fruit buds. This latter operation is best done immediately after the leaves fall.

PRUNING DIRECTIONS

PRUNING PIP FRUITS

With apples and pears, each variety shows an individual and very distinctive expansion of the tree framework from the branches and shoots, and varied types of fruit bud development. Basically, both are produced by the tree frameworks and pruning methods already set out on pages 12 to 16. However, certain varieties can be detailed individually as they are good examples of the different types which occur. Varieties such as Golden Delicious, Jonathan and James Grieve, as well as Beurre Alexandre Lucas – on dwarf stock – will produce a spindle type of tree without any well-defined central axis. This will happen unless earlier pruning has created a systematic production of lateral branches. They are more suitable for close planting and fruit heavily on one-year-old wood.

Varieties such as Cox Orange Pippin, Bramley's Seedling and Conference, naturally produce a wider framework. Their one-year-old shoots rarely carry fruit buds. Even when grafted on a dwarf stock, greater distances between the trees are needed. Such expansive frameworks are initially based on just a few laterals, the more upright shoots remaining as fruit branches. The laterals naturally form a wide angle to the central axis of the tree, provided they are not shortened. In this way the strong shoots are restricted and so earlier blossom production is encouraged. Alternatively, one can cut back the future leading branches as long as one bears in mind their strong shoots. Varieties difficult to harvest are those whose natural growth is very upright e.g. Doyenne du Comice and Doyenne Blanc Pears, and Cox on a strong stock. These can be pruned to give an additional suppression of shoot growth, with a resulting earlier production of fruit. In this case, one regulates a few laterals on the central axis to be horizontal within the branch scaffold structure of the tree.

Just as important as producing earlier fruiting on the young framework, is the need for adequate strength of the shoots within the growing framework and the maintenance of yielding ability, as well as their fixed maximum adjustment in the given standing space. Where numerous sprouts have been produced by hard pruning back of branches, one must be prepared to remove them by hand in the summer. On such trees, projecting and overcrowding branches must be sawn off.

The branch extensions are diverted to the more slanting, weaker laterals. Thus, the crop can be harvested easier from the ground level. Worn-out fruiting wood is removed in order to encourage the production of young fruiting wood.

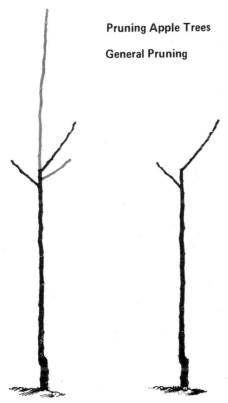

Pruning Apple Trees

General Pruning

Poorly Developed Grafts
As there are hardly any early shoots present from which the framework can be formed, the medium-strong early flowering branches must be encouraged. This is not produced by the pruning back of the strong centre shoot, but occurs because of the diversion to the weaker laterals; these are not cut back.

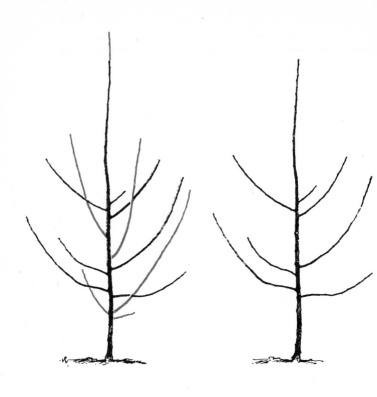

Well-developed One-Year-Old Grafts

The earliest shoots can be used for the framework structure. Laterals that are too numerous, close to the ground or too vertical and competing, should be removed. The remainder are not shortened. The main stem can be shortened slightly.

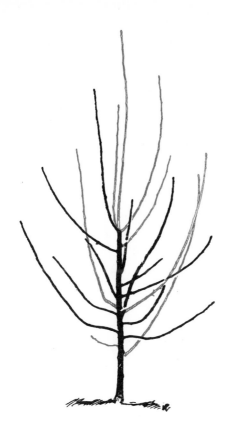

Well-developed Two-Year-Old Grafts

In a similar manner with a two-year-old graft, all the surplus shoots are removed. Instead of pruning back the top of the original central shoots, these shoots are diverted to a lateral. The horizontal, only medium strong laterals, are left alone and usually not shortened.

The less that the elongation of the central stem is cut
back, then the slimmer and narrower will be the tree
framework, and the wider becomes the branch angle
of the laterals to the main stem.

Golden Delicious Malling IX without Scaffold Structure - One Year after Planting

In this framework there is no definite lead branch, all branches are 'equal'. With no pruning back of the laterals, the framework base has grown more horizontally. At the top, only weak, slanting shoots have been produced. Apart from the removal of the competing lead shoot, and the shortening of the long laterals, no further pruning is required.

31

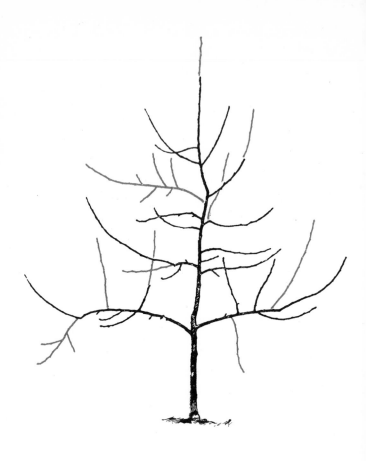

Golden Delicious Malling IX without Scaffold
Structure - Two Years after Planting
This has grown out of a narrow spindle shape into a
somewhat broader base with a definite central stem.

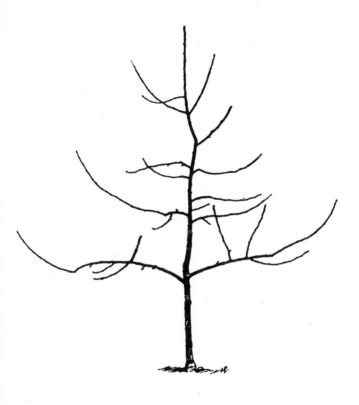

In this open framework, a strong lateral in the centre and some superfluous shoots have been removed. Only the one-year-old growth on the central stem has been cut back to stabilise it and to promote growth in the side shoots at the top of the framework. No further pruning back is necessary.

Golden Delicious Malling IX without Scaffold Structure - Three Years after Planting

This tree is so well balanced in its fruiting branch structure, that at this stage only slight pruning is necessary. Again, only tne central stem needs to be shortened.

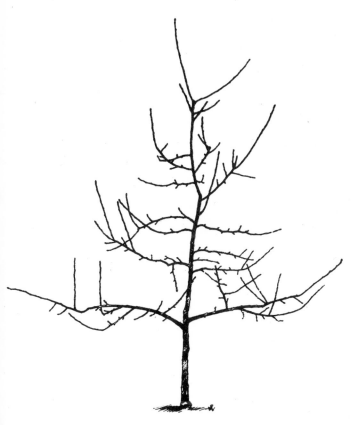

It is preferable for base branches to develop more strongly than other parts of the framework as they are the least exposed to light and are physiologically at a disadvantage to the upper parts of the tree. Thus, even in the young tree, overgrowth of the base of the framework can be prevented, and a foundation laid for the future fruit production on all parts of the tree.

Golden Delicious Malling IX without Scaffold
Structure - Fifteen Years after Planting
An example from a densely planted orchard with trees
arranged in a 10 x 8 ft (3 x 2.5m) layout. By repeated
and prompt removal of the stronger laterals up to the
main trunk, and by diverting the central shoots on
the more horizontal branches, a narrow, base-
orientated framework is created.

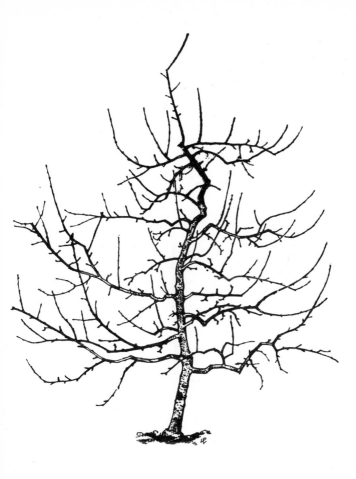

Projecting branches at the top of the framework have been removed, and the young shoots, also within the framework, have not been shortened. Old fruiting wood has been removed and the weak, younger growth adjusted by pruning back.

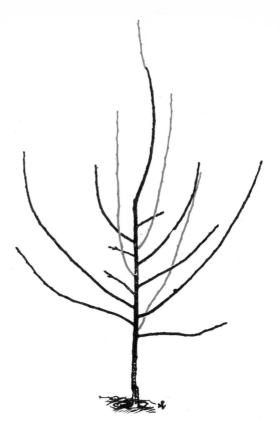

Cox Orange Malling IX with Scaffold Structure - One Year after Planting

The framework of the medium-strong growing Cox has one main shoot. This can soon be transformed into fruiting wood by retaining those weaker growing laterals growing at a shallow angle, to the main stem. Therefore, these laterals should not be shortened. Two early laterals, somewhat stronger and well placed, are also incorporated into the structure. The laterals considered suitable for the structure frame should be pruned lightly but only in the second growth year.

38

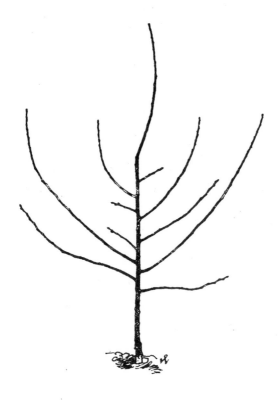

In a systematic building of the tree framework, the main stem and the over-developed laterals were moderately cut back and superfluous and vertical laterals were completely removed. All other laterals remain unpruned and assist the production of an early crop.

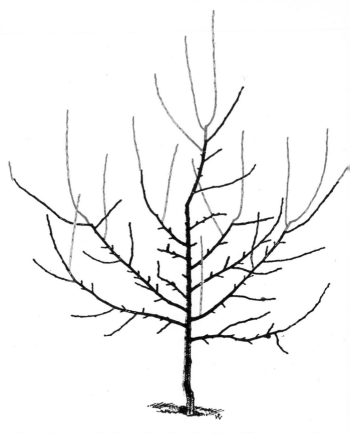

Cox Orange Malling IX with Scaffold Structure - Two
Years after Planting

The central stem and lateral lead branches, organised
from the previous year, stand out clearly from the
fruiting branches in this framework. By moderate
pruning back of the lead shoots, and careful treatment of other parts of the framework, numerous spur
shoots are produced. These are valuable in the formation of early flowering.

40

The central stem and leading laterals were shortened lightly, whilst the very strong and vertical growth was diverted to more horizontal and weaker shoots. Vertical shoots, which were overcrowding the framework, have been pruned back to the central stem. The fruiting wood remained unpruned.

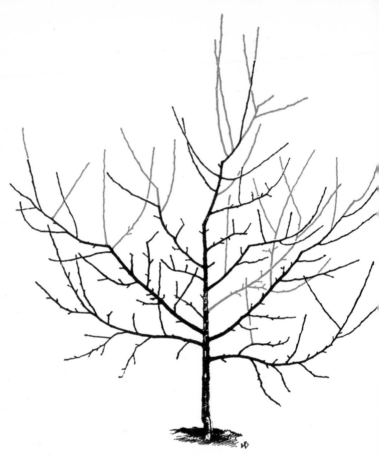

Cox Orange/Malling IX with Scaffold Structure -
Three Years after Planting

Through the stronger growth and development of
leading laterals, the whole framework becomes
broader than that of Golden Delicious on a similar
rootstock. Promotion of the base, together with
suppression of the tips of the framework and the
opening-up of the centre of the tree to let in the light,
must be started in young trees, at an early stage of
growth.

The basal laterals, both on the main framework and on the lead branches, remain unpruned. The tips of the central stem and lead laterals were pruned back to more horizontal shoots. These should only be slightly shortened, or not at all.

Cox Orange/Malling IX with Scaffold Structure -
Fifteen Years after Planting

An example taken from an orchard with a 10 x 10 ft
(3 x 3m) planting distance. The framework is broad-
oval in shape and shows clearly the more systematic
structure with two leading side branches, designed
from the outset for the maximum utilisation of the
available space. Cox needs a wider spacing and a
broader framework than Golden Delicious in order to
maintain older fruiting wood which is still productive.
First, one removes the stronger, projecting branches
at the ends of the framework and the overcrowding,
more vertical branches in the centre are removed.

Next, any strong young shoots are removed, and fruiting wood which is over 4—5 years old is either completely removed, or radically cut back.

When pruning is complete, the framework has the right balance between growth and fruiting wood. The base of the framework is not shaded by the upper branches, and is, in general, covered with fruit-producing short shoots or spurs. The upper part of the framework is so near the ground at about 8 ft (2.5 m) that it can be easily harvested.

46

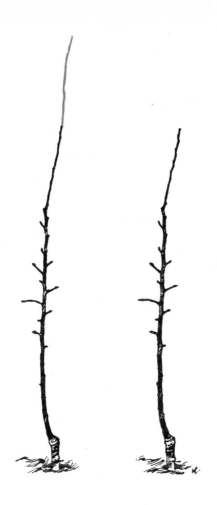

Boskoop/Malling IX - One Year after Planting

In the first year of growth Boskoop produces a long central shoot and isolated short laterals. In order to obtain a proportionate cover with only medium-strong branches, no pruning is needed other than to shorten the central stem as shown.

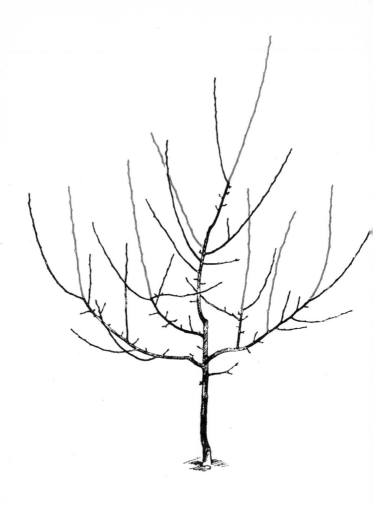

Boskoop/Malling IX - Two Years after Planting

Here is a framework developed from a two-year-old graft, with two leading laterals, which is a very open and well organised structure. A similar effect is possible with Bramley's Seedling.

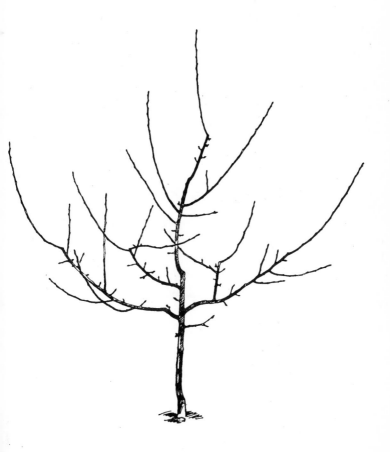

Young shoots which were growing vertically and were too strongly developed, have been removed to the branch node. Young shoots on the main growth structure and fruit branches have not been shortened.

49

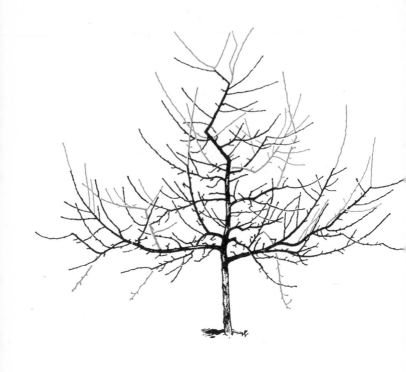

Boskoop/Malling IX - Ten Years after Planting

This is the proper development of a tree from a dense orchard planted out with 13 x 6 ft (4 x 2m) spacing. In a densely planted orchard, the naturally strong growth of Boskoop can be modified by reasonable encouragement of the base of the framework. However, this part of the tree tends to be shaded by the upper branches.

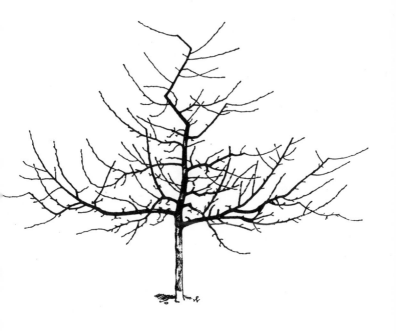

In spite of the advantages associated with this type of structure, some correction by pruning was necessary. Any overcrowding of the framework base and top has been eliminated together with any congestion of vertical branches and young shoots. The old fruiting wood was shortened.

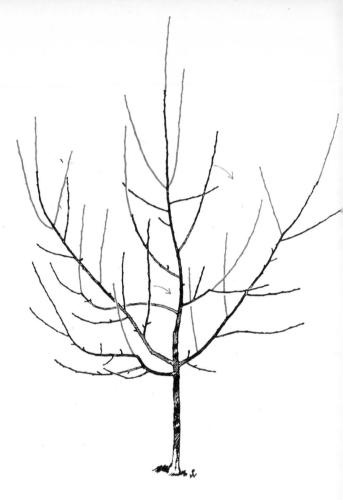

Golden Delicious/Malling IV with Scaffold Structure -
Two Years after Planting

On the stronger growing rootstock Malling IV,
Golden Delicious shows considerably more vigorous
growth than on the dwarf stock Malling IX (see p.32).
The basic framework for shoot-producing leading
laterals is of the same pattern as that described for
Cox/Malling IX with a scaffold structure (see p.40).

Those one-year-old shoots which grew too vertically
or were too numerous, have been either removed or
separately tied back into a horizontal position. The
shoots then develop into fruiting branches much
sooner. The main stem and the leading laterals have
also been shortened.

53

Golden Delicious/Malling IV with Scaffold Structure -
Three Years after Planting

This framework has developed satisfactorily and is
well spread out. The left-hand leading lateral shows
vigorous growth and is already upsetting the overall
balance of the framework. Long shoots tied into a
horizontal position the previous year have already
produced flower buds.

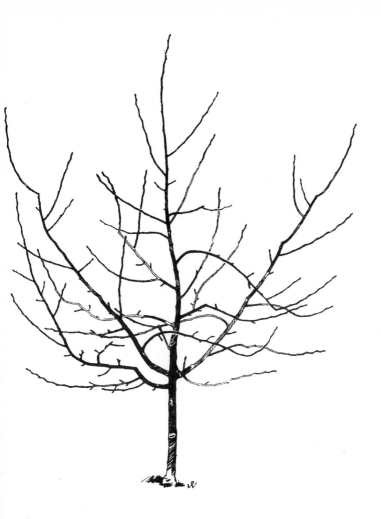

Here the surplus sprouts have been removed on the left-hand lateral. Extension growth of the lateral was diverted to a rather weaker, more horizontal young shoot. The right-hand lateral was cut back to approximately the same height as the left-hand one. No further pruning back was necessary at this stage.

Golden Delicious/Malling IV with Scaffold Structure -
Four Years after Planting

This framework has become too high for the crop to
be picked easily. The upper parts of the framework
have started to congest the centre of the tree. Too
many young shoots have been produced as a result of
earlier severe thinning out and heavy pruning back of
the leading branches.

The central stem and the laterals have been cut back to horizontal, but weaker shoots which have not been shortened and very thick branches were either removed or diverted. Young shoots are then restricted to weaker and more slanting branches. Fruiting wood which is too old (3 years for Golden Delicious, 4–5 years for Cox and Boskoop) must now be removed for growth re-generation.

Reduction of a Fifteen-Year-Old Golden Delicious/
Malling IV Framework
The framework must be formed in such a manner
that its height and breadth leave enough room to
work between the trees. The fruiting area is thus kept
close to the ground, and light can reach the centre of
the framework. To begin with, branches overhanging
or projecting into the working lane should be
removed or diverted.

58

Next, the inter-twining thinner branches — particularly in the upper framework — are removed or reduced in length. If young sprouts are too numerous, most are cut out. At the base of the tree, the older and shaded fruiting branches, which produce inferior apples, are either removed or cut back to half their length.

59

The overall pruning, which was quite severe in parts, produces a close-to-the-ground, light, airy and well balanced framework. Since this severe pruning leads to a strong production of new shoots, systematic follow-up treatment must be applied for several years. This should begin with the tearing-off of all the vertical sprouts in summer (see p.20).

Treatment of Old, Single Branches

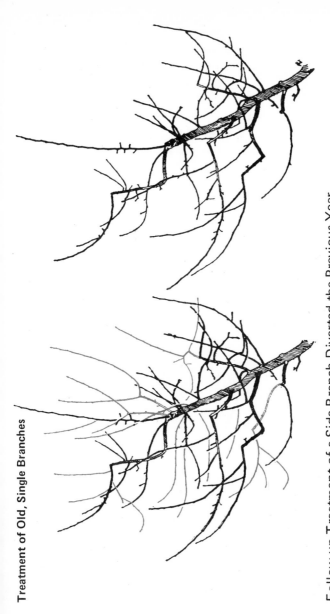

Follow-up Treatment of a Side Branch Diverted the Previous Year

All shoots and branches which grow too vertical or too dense, are removed. Of the remaining young shoots, neither those producing length nor foliage are shortened.

Control Pruning on a Low Branch

The foundation structure of the whole framework is in approximately its sixth year of growth. The correct balance between the base and the top has been achieved and so control pruning can commence. To begin with, the inner and the vertical shoots are cut back flush to the branch.

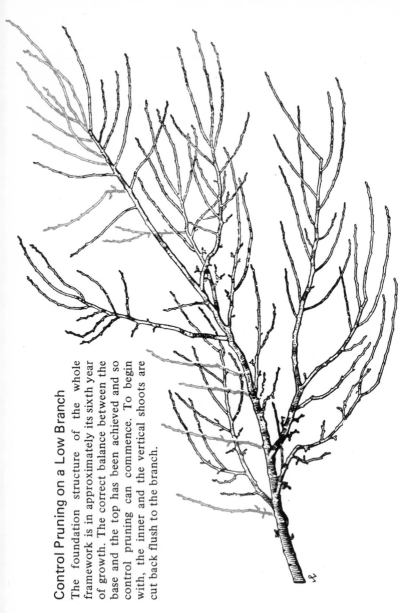

The next stage is to remove those shoots which overlap and are too dense.

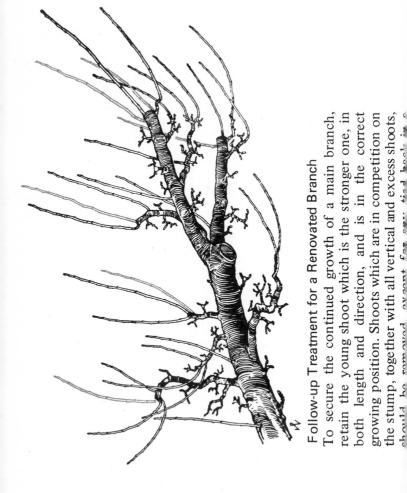

Follow-up Treatment for a Renovated Branch

To secure the continued growth of a main branch,
retain the young shoot which is the stronger one, in
both length and direction, and is in the correct
growing position. Shoots which are in competition on
the stump, together with all vertical and excess shoots,
should be removed, except for any tied back in a

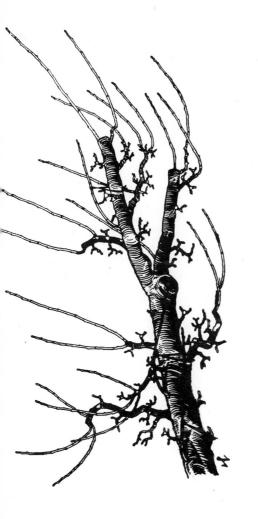

Both for promotion of sufficient foliage, and creation of fruiting wood, the remaining young shoots are given special follow-up treatment. Neither those that are tied nor those naturally horizontal are shortened to promote fruit buds.

Control Pruning on a Strong-growing, Free-standing
Framework at the Cropping Stage

The expanding framework of this four-branched tree
is fairly favourably shaped with a reasonable distance
between the branches, thus avoiding a whorl situation.

After the removal of the overcrowding branches, the young shoots of the centre stem and main branches were diverted. The young shoots were not shortened. With an expanded framework which is produced in this way there is a very considerable increase in pruning and harvesting costs compared with a low framework on the weaker stock Malling IX.

Cox Orange Framework too High and Wide after
Twelve Years Growth

The essential hard pruning shown here is best spread
over a few years. In the first year, saw off all branches
projecting into the cultivation lane, together with
those which upset the framework balance. Further,
the numerous young sprouts which grow around the
pruning wounds in the summer are useless and should
be removed immediately.

In the second year, remove branches which are
causing overcrowding, together with any one-year-old
shoots resulting from the previous year's pruning.

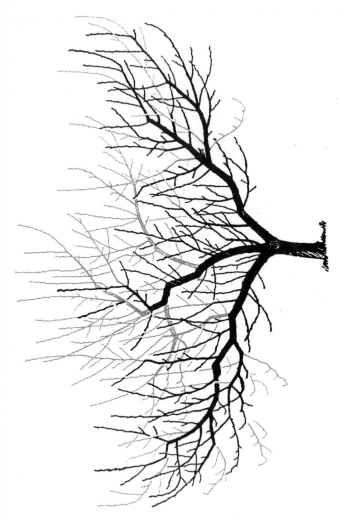

In the upper part of the framework, many young shoots have again been produced, so in the third year, pruning surgery is again necessary, and the stronger branches on the upper part of the trunk must be sawn off. Some of the vertical young shoots should also be removed in summer and older fruiting wood on the base branches can be cut out or

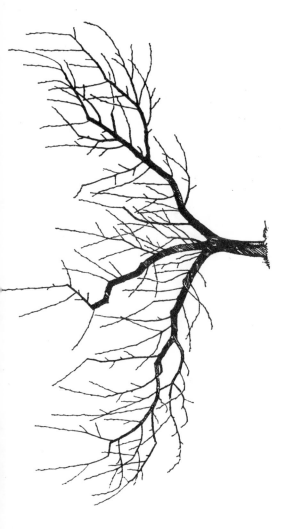

Thus a low framework is produced with young fruiting wood all the way around. By vigorous shortening and thinning out of the trunk we have achieved a physiological balance between the base and the top. This rather flattened tree also leaves enough space for working in the cultivation lane.

71

Transplanted Fifteen-Year-Old Cox/Malling IX - Two
Years in New Site

To encourage growth, the tree framework is only
gently pruned when replanting. Now some large
branches overshadow the base of the tree, so hard
pruning is needed.

72

A leading lateral has now been removed to keep the cultivation lane clear and two overhanging and flattened branches at the top have also been sawn off. On the remaining branches in the low structure, only the young sprouts and old fruiting wood have been cut away.

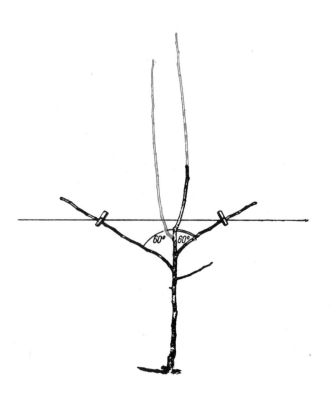

One Year Framework

In marked contrast to the spindle type of tree, the central shoot must be sharply pruned back. This will benefit the laterals, which need to be only slightly shortened. Fasten the laterals on to the supporting wire at an angle of 60° to the centre stem as shown.

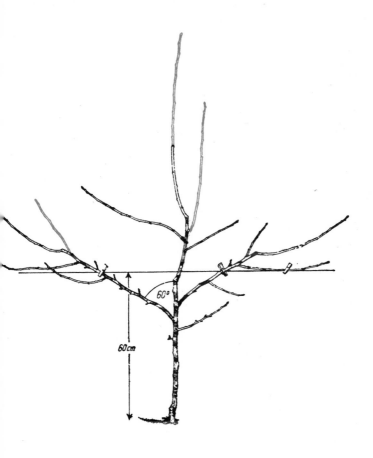

Two Year Framework

In the following year, cut back the centre stem to about half its new growth, and remove any young competing shoots. Tie the strong side shoots to the supporting wire in mid-summer as shown and do not prune back in the autumn.

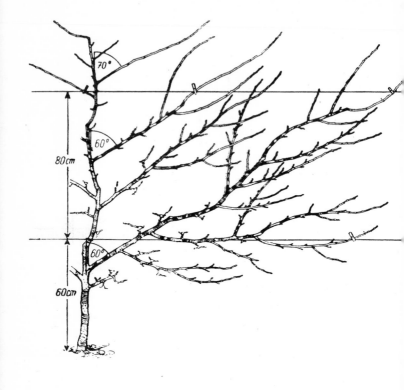

Four Year Framework

By appropriate growth of the laterals, higher tiers are developed in subsequent years. The laterals at the base must maintain a greater growth rate at the expense of the top branches. Because of the tendency to horizontal growth, the danger of their barrenness is reduced.

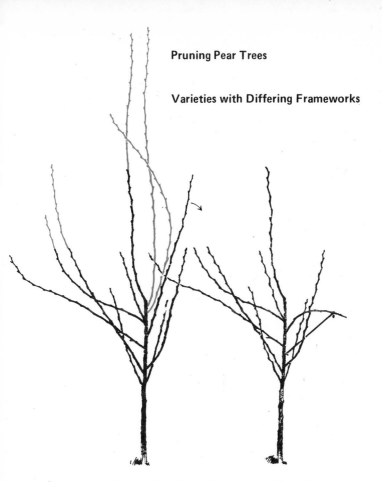

Varieties with Differing Frameworks

Lucas/Quince without Scaffold Structure - One Year after Planting

Remove all laterals which are vertical and growing vigorously. Isolated branches should be tied horizontally, without pruning, in order to promote fruit bud production. The over-long centre stem has to be sufficiently shortened to keep its balance with the laterals. Specific structure branches are not being developed.

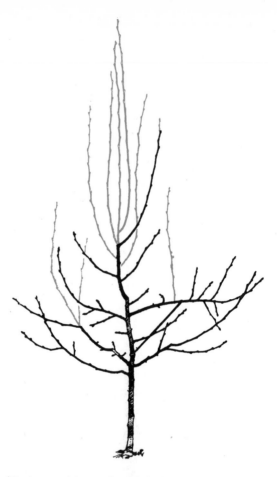

Lucas/Quince without Scaffold Structure - Two Years
after Planting
Development of fruit buds in pears commences on
the base branches, which are covered with short
shoots. By leaving the growth of the centre stem
untouched, it is possible to influence the top growth
and prevent the physiologically weaker base of the
framework becoming overwhelmed.

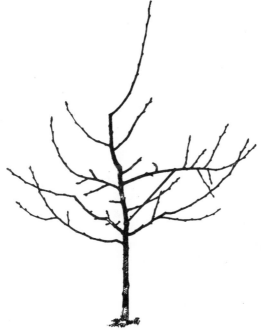

By redirecting the growth and by tying back in a horizontal plane, fruit bud promotion is encouraged in the lower parts of the tree's framework. Upright shoots on the basal laterals were removed, as were the vertical top shoots, and thus the main stem continues its growth on a weak and slanting growth shoot. Removal of the competing shoots has secured the main stem growth. This was only very lightly pruned back.

Lucas/Quince without Scaffold Structure - Five Years after Planting

This tree has already ceased producing any further shoot growth. A few branches and young, vertical shoots upset the overall balance both in the upper and lower parts of the tree. The development of weaker, more slanting laterals guarantees quicker production of more abundant blossom.

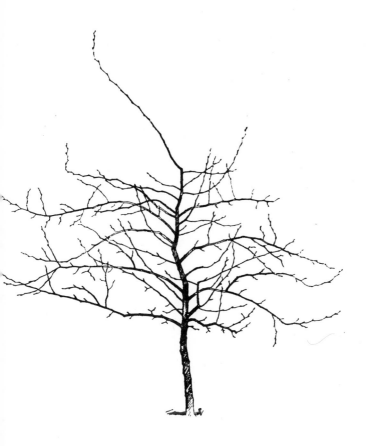

Overcrowding branches have been removed together
with the stronger vertical shoots at the top of the
framework and other isolated vertical shoots. Isolated,
old and barren fruit branches had already been
pruned out.

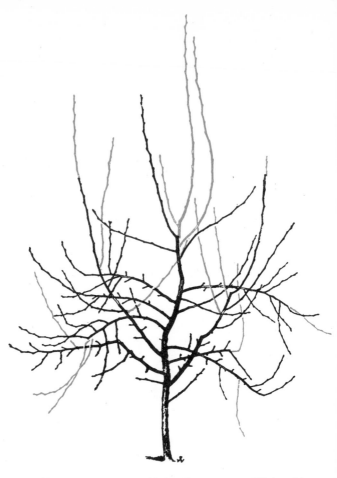

Lucas/Quince with Scaffold Structure - Three Years
after Planting

In contrast to the preceding frameworks, the laterals
here have been encouraged to become the leading
branches. They are clearly distinguished from the rest
of the unpruned cropping branches by their more
vertical growth. This kind of growth pattern is possible with a round and flat framework.

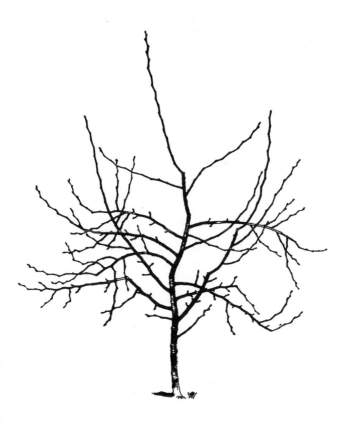

The centre stem here has been diverted on to a lower, young shoot and slightly shortened. All narrow forking and screening shoots have been removed from both leading laterals, which were pruned back to the same height.

Lucas/Quince as a Flat Framework - Ten Years after
Planting
Here is a recognisably clearer framework, produced
from a weak centre stem and fairly flat, strong lateral
lead branches. All the rest are fruiting branches, but
their fruit-wood is so weakened, partly by previous
cropping, that it will be necessary to shorten them to
encourage new growth.

84

The pruning surgery required here in this extensive but well-balanced framework is relatively light. By a further restriction of the structure frame on the centre stem, any projection and subsequent shading of the lower framework is prevented. Sprouts need to be cut back and the weaker two-year-old, together with the more vertical fruiting branches must be shortened on all parts of the framework.

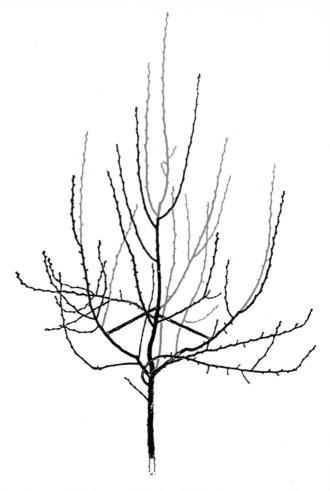

Conference/Quince with Scaffold Structure - Three Years after Planting

In contrast to Lucas, this variety grows more strongly and in a more upright manner. The hardest part of framework training is made easier by a systematic approach and the occasional use of branch spreaders and ties can be of considerable assistance.

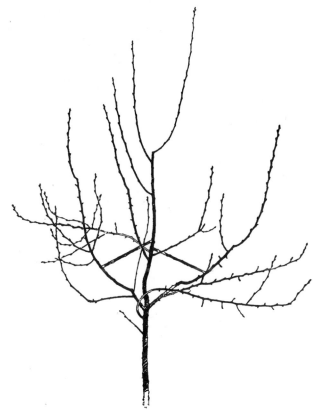

Also in this case, the central stem was checked in its
growth by diversion and the vertical shoots and
sprouts were cut back completely. Further, by
spreading them, any upright growth of the vertical
laterals has been checked. Only the leading young
laterals need to be pruned back a little if necessary. In
order to promote the formation of fruit buds, isolated and rather weaker one-year-old twigs in the
framework were left unpruned and not shortened
until the second year after blooming. They were then
pruned to half their length.

Conference/Quince with Scaffold Structure - after Ten Years

In the previous year the branches in the upper framework had been cut back considerably. This led to the stronger development of young shoots in this area. Further restriction of growth is essential in order to encourage the development and production of a framework close to the ground.

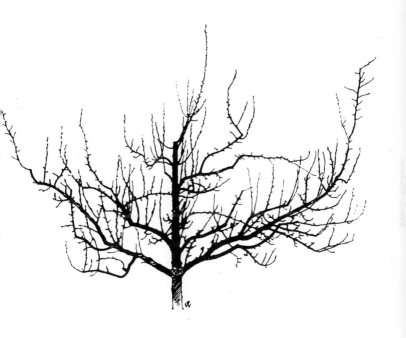

Removal of the overcrowding branches on the old
growth must be followed immediately by the removal
of all the soft sprouts. If this is done at the right time
in summer, their strong growth can be prevented (see
p.20). The shortening of the two-year-old fruiting
branches to about half their length is important if
there is to be early fruit production.

89

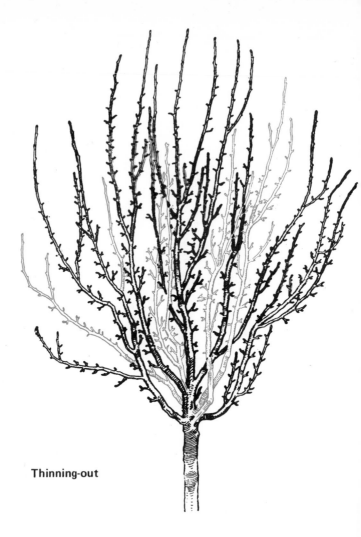

Thinning-out

Thinning-out an Unpruned Young Pear Framework
After removing the overcrowding main branches, any
other branches which cross or rub against others are
either completely cut out or cut back to fruiting
wood length.

Finally, a light pruning back (possibly to older wood) is carried out on branches which are too long. Between the tips and the base there should be an angle of 90° for pear trees. For apples, sweet cherries and plums, an angle of 120° should be aimed for. The upper leading laterals then become suitably spread out.

With thinning, it is most important to cut out isolated large branches. This will provide enough light for the whole framework and encourage new growth.

PRUNING STONE FRUIT

As far as the structure of the framework is concerned, the same basic principles apply as for pip fruit. Since the lateral branches develop much more weakly than on apple and pear trees, one can develop more of them at an earlier stage. In addition to the main stem, there can be four of them with plums, morello cherry and peaches and five with sweet cherries, yellow plums and apricots. Lateral shoots which are not required for the general structure, can then be left without any pruning back, to encourage early fruiting in the young framework, provided that they are secondary to the leading laterals by being more horizontal or slanting. The formation of a flattened framework, as seen in the illustration pp. 100–101, is feasible with morello cherries, peaches and apricots. After the completion of the framework structure, early fruiting varieties of plum and Mirabelles (yellow plums), and more particularly morello cherries and peaches, should undergo an overall, general pruning for the maintenance and development of stronger young shoots and larger fruit (even on the lower framework). All over-crowding, non-productive and pendulous branches should also be removed, as and when necessary.

Sweet cherries and a few naturally sour cherries need very little pruning after the framework structure has been formed. With peach trees, the year after thinning out, the young shoots and the fruiting wood should be cut back in order to restrict the amount of blossom and thereby encourage the production of larger fruit.

All stone fruit types and varieties may require renovating pruning as in the examples on pp. 106–108. Then, in spite of increased fertilisation, a pronounced deterioration in growth sets in with a noticeable decline in production of young shoots and fruit.

Morello Cherry

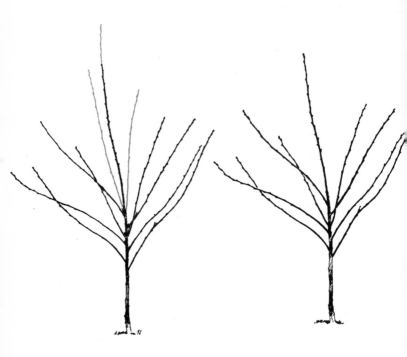

Pruning One-Year-Old Morello Cherry

The framework of the morello cherry needs to be as close to the ground as possible so that the cherry crop can be easily picked. Thus the shoots at the base of the trunk, and the more slanting shoots, must be retained. Only the centre shoot is lightly pruned back. This type of pruning in the first year encourages the proper development of the tree.

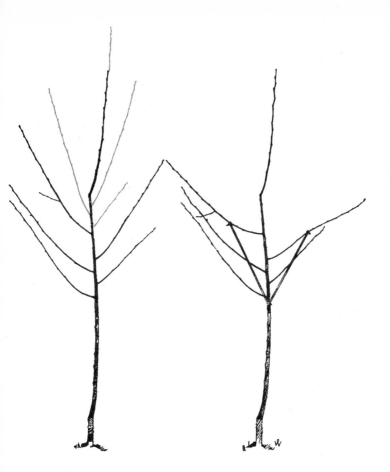

Pruning Two-Year-Old Morello Cherry

The simple structure of the two-year-old framework
has widely spaced laterals. Vertical, competitive
shoots are completely removed. In special cases
vertical laterals can be tied back more horizontally.
By this type of pruning, a broader framework is
produced. Top development is restricted by diversion
of growth on to one main branch, which is not
shortened at all.

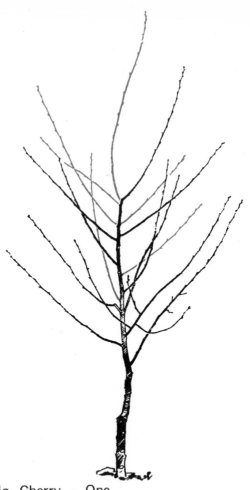

Morello Cherry - One
Year after Planting

The young framework from p.95 is shown here more
favourably developed. The laterals are so well spaced
on the main stem that they do not crowd each other.
Pruning is seldom needed when the laterals grow at
the proper angle to the centre stem.

96

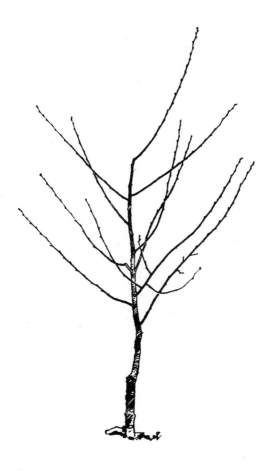

As with pip fruit, the central stem must be diverted. Any side shoots which are competing with the new central stem have been removed, together with any shoots causing overcrowding in the centre of the framework.

Round Framework of Morello Cherry - Five Years after Planting

On pages 98–101, the various types of round and flat frameworks of trees of the same age are illustrated. The round framework is shown with a pronounced central axis and three lateral lead branches. On these, many-branching parts of the framework have developed.

Here, the central stem and laterals were diverted to
more horizontal elongations of shoots. Any competing shoots were removed on principle. Any young
shoots causing overcrowding, particularly in the
upper part of the framework, were cut out, as was the
older, non-productive wood. The time-consuming
work of shortening young shoots is not recommended,
since morello cherries which are pruned severely
produce an inferior crop.

Flat Framework of Morello Cherry - Five Years after Planting

Of all the stone fruits, the morello cherry is the easiest to establish and maintain as a flat framework. It is illustrated here with only two leading laterals. The central stem barely stands any higher than the laterals. A definite reduction of the upper framework is required. This can be achieved by diverting some branches and removing young shoots, as necessary, in order to let enough light into the centre of the tree and to enable the fruit to be picked easily without any obstructions.

100

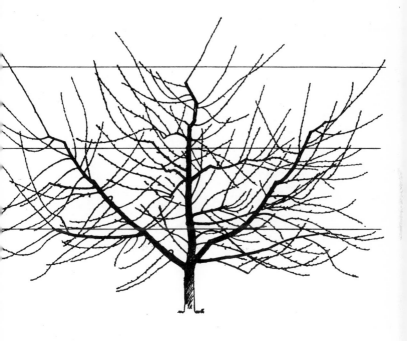

In addition to the diversion of branches, vertical young shoots on the upper side of the leading laterals must also be removed. At the base, any old, unproductive fruit wood should either be pruned back to produce new growth or removed completely. The previous practice of pruning back young shoots is no longer carried out.

Lightly Pruned Morello Cherry - Ten Years after Planting
This framework was pruned for the first time after 5 years growth. At that stage the trunk was shortened, and the vertical, isolated laterals removed.

This is the framework after 10 years, following extensive management of the lower structure. Again some branches in the inner framework were removed, as were all unproductive fruit branches and over-crowding young shoots.

Unpruned Morello Cherry - Ten Years after Planting
The completely unpruned, and by now too dense and
too old, framework produced high yields of poor
quality fruit which was very difficult to pick. It is in a
completely enclosed canopy, and could only be
renovated by very hard pruning surgery.

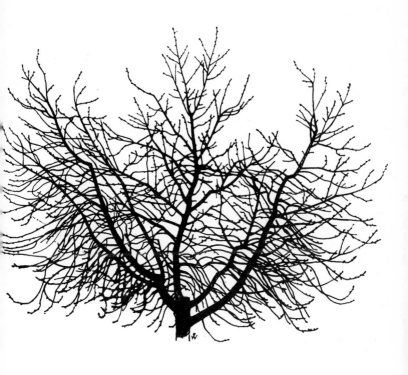

In the first year of treatment, all the unwanted over-crowding large branches were removed, particularly from the centre of this tree. The main rising trunk was taken out in order to produce a hollow frame-work. This tree surgery will immediately stimulate young shoot development. A further pruning in the second year follows, similar to that illustrated on p.103.

Renovating a Moderately Unproductive Branch

Overcrowding and hanging forked branches with unproductive shoots should be removed and vertical shoots retained for the future structure.

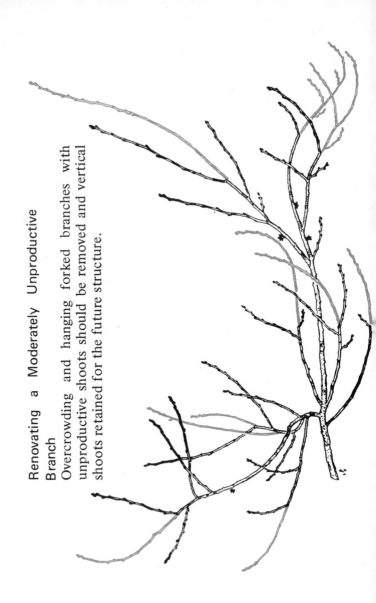

Follow-up Treatment of a Renovated Branch
Following pruning back, there is very strong growth
in all parts of the framework and unproductiveness is
quickly eliminated. Any surplus and badly spaced
shoots should be removed.

107

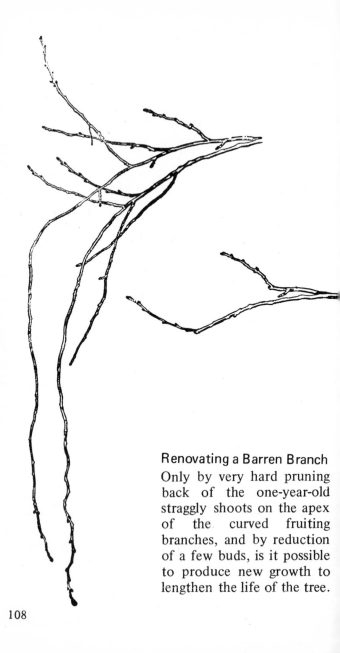

Renovating a Barren Branch
Only by very hard pruning back of the one-year-old straggly shoots on the apex of the curved fruiting branches, and by reduction of a few buds, is it possible to produce new growth to lengthen the life of the tree.

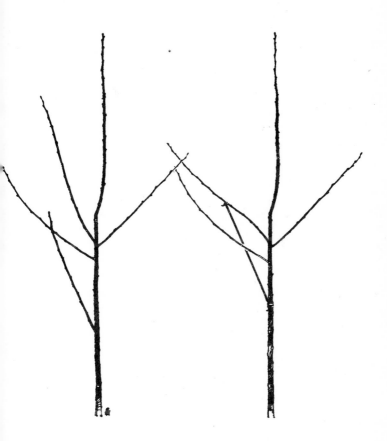

Sweet Cherry - One Year after Planting

This framework shows an untidy distribution of lead shoots. The vertical side-shoot can be tied back into a slanting position. In order to encourage a more horizontal growth of the laterals, the young shoots are left unpruned.

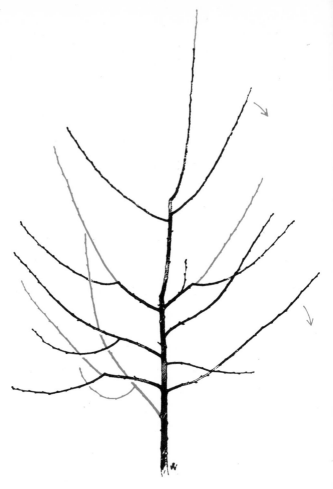

Sweet Cherry - Three Years after Planting

The framework has developed further. It now needs only light pruning. Since the central shoots have not been pruned back, the normally abundant vertical shoots fail to appear. These would later get in the way as thicker branches, and then produce a light gummy discharge.

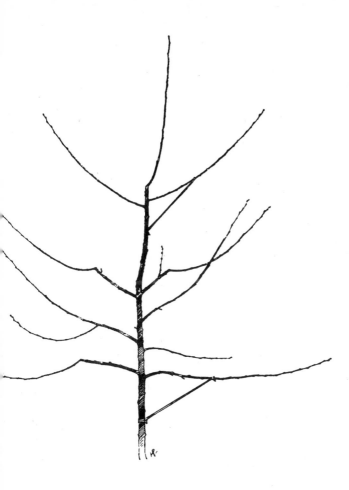

In order to secure a flatter branching, shoots which were too vertical have been diverted more horizontally, or in some instances, tied down. The lead shoot has been shortened, being too long.

Pruning Peach Trees

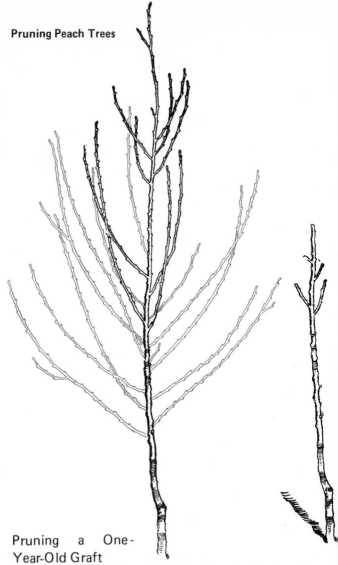

Pruning a One-
Year-Old Graft

The pruning can be carried out in a similar manner to
morello cherry (see p.94). Premature shoots at the
base of the stem are best removed. It is also possible
to shorten the remainder of the framework, as shown
on the right.

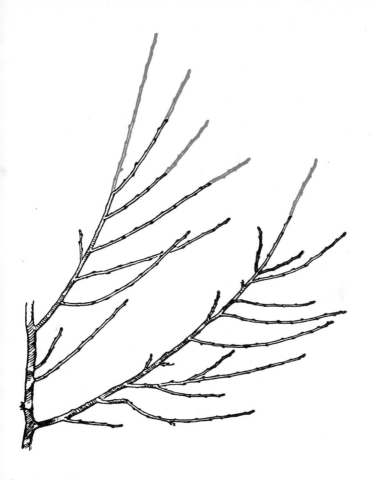

Pruning a Young and Unproductive Framework

To encourage early fruiting on young trees, those shoots which are not essential for the framework structure, particularly those at the base of the branches, should not be pruned. At the onset of sterility, particularly if it is severe, it is essential to prune the fruiting wood severely in early spring.

REGRAFTING

This method of shoot renewal involves replacement by grafting of a considerable part of the original tree framework by another variety.

The regrafting must be carefully planned, and only carried out if the tree is still healthy. However, the effort can be amply rewarded by subsequent crops. Very old trees and those in poor sites for fruit production are unsuitable for regrafting. Regrafting is carried out more frequently on apple and pear than with plum and cherry, or even apricot and peach. With the exception of peach, where only bud grafting is successful, all the remaining fruits are usually scion grafted.

From the many grafting methods which have been developed over the years, the only ones to become really well established are those that will definitely produce growth by simple techniques. Only compatible varieties are grafted, i.e. those which will grow with each other. The most satisfactory result is obtained when the grafted variety is stronger growing than the stock on which it is grafted.

The work is carried out as follows: Cut the scions and store them in a sufficiently cool, frost-proof place towards the end of December or in early January. Cut down the old tree framework in late winter to the middle of March. Re-cut the stump of the old tree immediately before grafting between mid-March and the end of May. (The actual time is decided by the behaviour of the graft scion.) Follow-up treatment of the graft stock and scions commences in the first summer and is essential until the structure of the new framework is established.

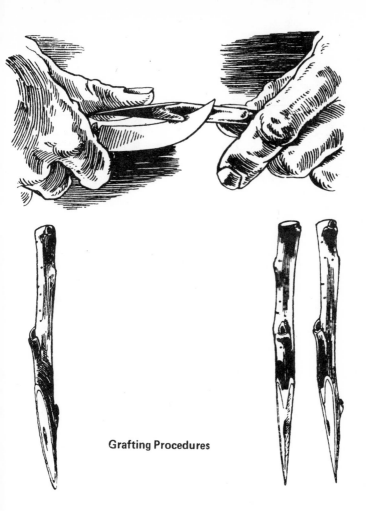

Grafting Procedures

Crown Grafting

Shape the scion with two slanting cuts towards each other, making an even-sided wedge, 1–1½in (3-4 cm) long, with the bud nearly at the top end in the middle opposite the cuts, i.e. on the third side. Remove a part of the bark on the wedge below the bud.

With the same pruning knife, make an identically shaped cut in the stock.

Insert the scion into the cut in the stock so that all the exposed surfaces of the stock and scion are in contact. In order to encourage healing of the cut surfaces, expose that on the scion very slightly, about 1/8 in (3-4 mm.) The lower bud on the graft should be at least 3/8 in (5mm) below the upper edge of the stock.

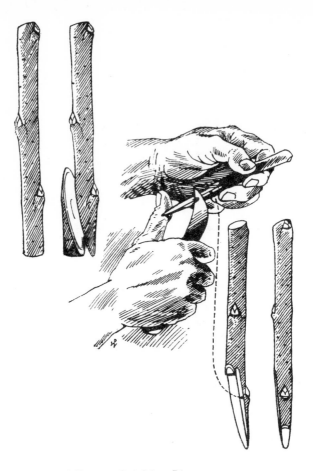

Improved Crown Grafting Plugs

A small horizontal cut is made almost at the top of
the normal joint. This is followed by a vertical cut,
thus making a small bridge in the graft which will
rest on the stock. This increases the contact surfaces
between scion and stock. The bark is then cut away
below the bridge on both sides of the cut surface, and
at the tip, as illustrated.

118

A cut about 1½in (4cm) long is made in the bark of
the stock, starting at the bottom and cutting upwards.
The bark is then loosened from the top downwards,
and this commences the joining surface on the stock.
The scion is inserted into the cut up to the bridge.
The lower bud on the graft must be at least 3/8in
(5mm) below the upper edge of the stock.

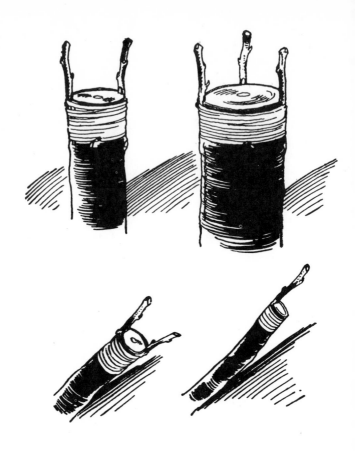

Graft Position on the Stock Head

The position of the grafts on the stock depends upon
the position of the branch and the required number
of scions. With an upright stock or branch, even
spacing is usual. With a slanting branch, one scion
only is used on the upper edge of stock, up to 1½in
(4cm) in diameter. If the stock is of 1½–2¼in
(4 to 6cm) diameter then two scions, one above and
one under, are used.

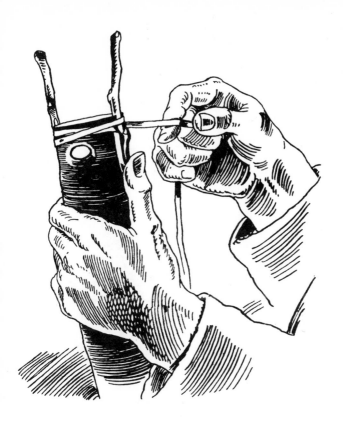

Binding and Sealing

Starting at the top, the binding of tape or raffia is wound around the head of the stock and over the scions, until the scion within the stock is completely bound over.

In order to avoid drying out of wound surfaces, and to keep out air and moisture, all exposed wounds and cut surfaces on both scion and stock should be immediately and completely covered with tree or grafting wax.

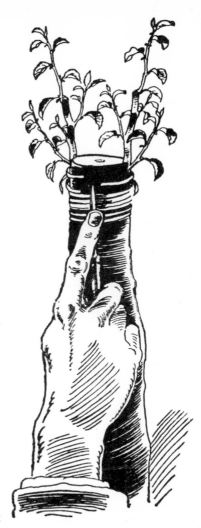

Treatment of the Stock
the Following Summer

The bindings must be cut away as soon as the grafts
are growing to prevent any strangling of the growth.
To encourage the growth of the grafts, all shoots on
the upper 12in (30cm) of the stock are removed.

Preparation of the Newly Grafted Framework
With the exception of essential supporting branches
(sap pullers) of the stock, all the main shoots forming
the future structure should be pruned back to an
outward-pointing bud as shown.

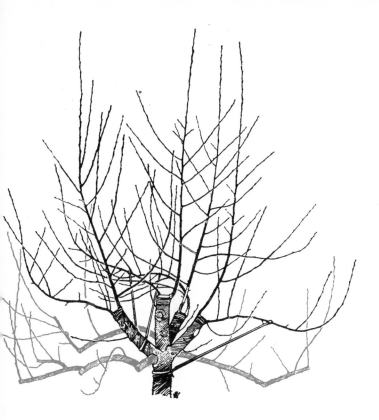

Treatment of Regrafted Framework after One Year's Development

During the growing season, there is very rapid growth of the sap pullers or supporting branches and the newly grafted scions. In the summer, one of the two grafts on each stock is tied back horizontally in order to develop the formation of early fruiting wood. In the winter, all the supporting branches of the stock should be sawn off, right back to the tree trunk, so that the developing framework is able to benefit from the whole of the sap stream.

Sometimes a scion develops a strong branch which can be used as the main stem. The tied-down and horizontally growing branches should be kept weaker since it is on them that the early fruit buds are formed. Without this spreading growth from the young shoots, developing branches would grow too densely and upright from the very start.

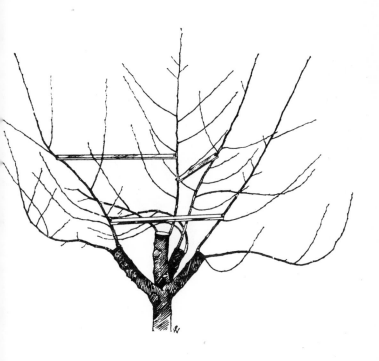

Here the strongest and most upright of the very numerous early shoots have been cut away so that the growth of the centre shoots can project above the side branches. Growth of the laterals must be cut to a common height by means of growth diversion. On the horizontal fruit branches the one-year-old growth is not shortened.

127

Reconstruction of a Regraft after Four Years Development

The re-development of a framework following a regrafting occurs quicker than that of a young tree. It starts out as a scaffold structure with fruiting branches. Pruning is of importance in order that the leading laterals can be diverted to grow less vertically whilst the more horizontal shoots are left intact on the fruit branches.

PRUNING BERRY FRUIT

The shrubby growth of gooseberries and currants is produced from shoot buds at the base of the stem. These develop evenly into the shoots of the bushes and shoot renewal continues from the root stock. The fruiting wood is usually more than one year old, and the best fruit is carried on second and third year wood.

Raspberries form single shoots or canes, which, in the second year, produce short lateral shoots with the flower buds. The canes always die back after two years but initially they grow out from shoot buds on the root crown like blackberries. Blackberry shoots themselves are productive for several years, but the early shoots can produce blossom in the first year — although it is usually in the second year that the short blossom shoots are produced from the main stem. There is still no general agreement about the necessity and method for pruning berry fruit. With gooseberries, it is essential to thin out the old fruit wood and prune back any young growth attacked by mildew. Currants must be thinned out when they are not producing sufficient fruiting wood. With raspberries, all the dying canes must be removed each year.

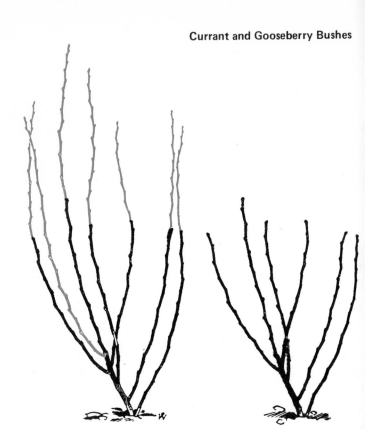

Growth Pruning a Currant Bush

Depending upon the variety, currant bushes have 3–5,
5–8 or 8–12 shoots. Only about 6 strong one-year-
old shoots are needed for a good scaffold structure.
Weak and overcrowding shoots should be removed.
With the less vigorous-growing redcurrant, reduce the
shoot length to about half — with the stronger ones
cut back to about a third — so that all shoots are
about the same height. Blackcurrants are often not
pruned back at all.

Fruit Wood Pruning

Young blackcurrant shoots need not be shortened. However, fruit wood pruning (i.e. cutting back some of the shoots) is often carried out with redcurrants, but only when there is insufficient fruiting wood on the other shoots.

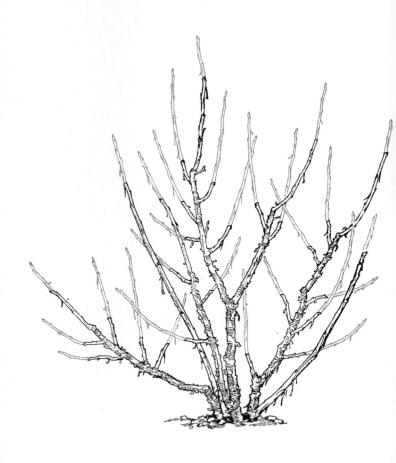

In order to improve the fruit quality, give both bush and espalier currants a fairly hard pruning of the fruit wood as indicated.

132

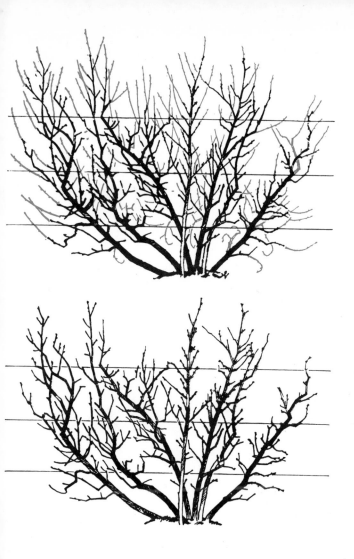

Fruit Wood Pruning of an Espalier Redcurrant
This pruning consists of the removal of the old
structural branches, diversion of the lower laterals,
and individual shortening of young shoots.

133

On gooseberry bushes, a pruning of the fruit wood should first be carried out to promote both further growth and fruit size. The second aim of pruning is to remove shoot tips which are infected with mildew.

The branch shown here was pruned back in the preceding year, and so the number of shoots is now limited to those which are necessary. The shoots are shortened by nearly one third.

Thinning-out Gooseberry and Currant Bushes

Berry bushes are often too thick and dense. They
have too much dark-coloured old growth which
produces only a few small fruits and a multitude of
weak young shoots from the base. The main object of
such thinning out is to leave only 6—8 main branches
and no fruit wood over 3 years old.

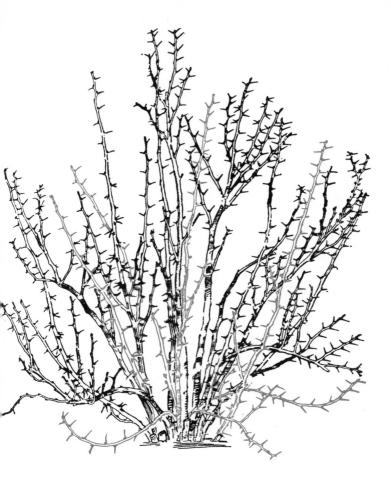

To protect yourself from injury from the thorns, use a branch knife with a long handle to remove the old wood near the ground. A sufficient number of vigorous healthy light coloured, young shoots growing from the rootstock, are left to replenish the structure of the bush, i.e. as replacement for the older wood which has been removed.

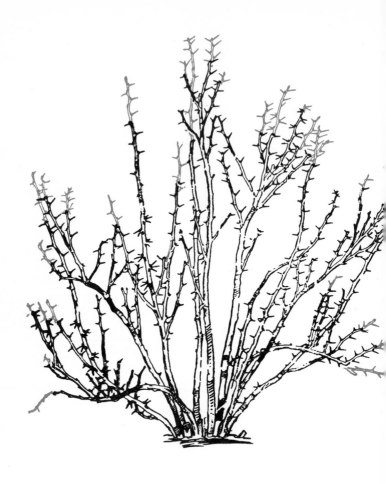

All the long, one-year-old shoots should be shortened by about one third, particularly when the tips are attacked by gooseberry mildew.

Pruning Raspberries

To encourage growth and production of root suckers, newly planted raspberries in moist soil can be cut back to a height of about 20 in (50cm), whilst in dry conditions they are cut down to just above soil level. All two-year-old canes, which die off naturally, should be cut down to soil level as shown, immediately fruiting has finished. This checks the spread of the raspberry stunt virus, which starts from these canes.

Pruning Thornless Blackberries as a Hedge

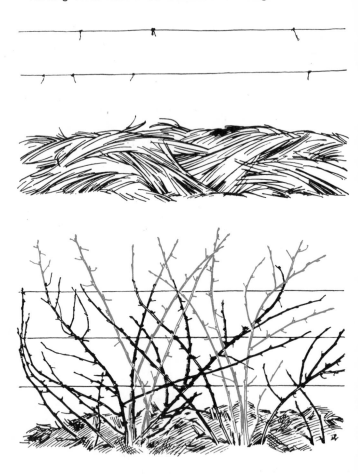

One-year-old runners lying on the ground are suscep-
tible to frost. Therefore, in winter they should be
covered with a thin layer of straw. In spring cut away
the old branches and tie up the young shoots high on
the wires to make a new trellis or hedge.

PRUNING GRAPE VINES

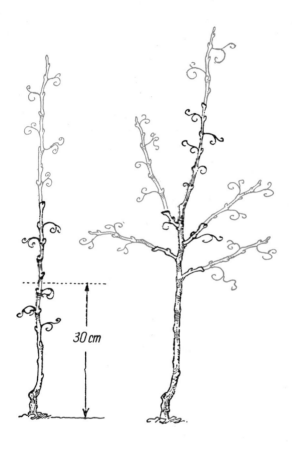

30 cm

One year after planting, the main vine should be shortened to about 12in (30cm) and six buds. In the following year cut back the laterals to two buds and the lead shoot to six buds.

Varieties which produce weak shoots and short wood
growth should be given a spur pruning, i.e. cut back
all laterals to two buds, in late winter/early spring.

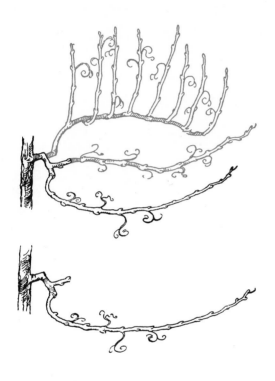

The arch vine pruning method should be used on those varieties with strong growth and elongated fruiting wood.

TYPE AND TIME OF PRUNING

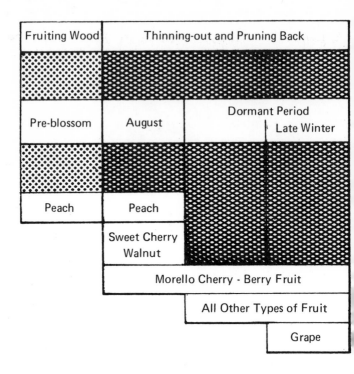

Fruiting Wood	Thinning-out and Pruning Back		
░░░░░	▓▓▓▓▓▓▓▓▓▓▓▓▓▓▓▓▓▓		
Pre-blossom	August	Dormant Period	Late Winter
░░░░░	▓▓▓▓	▓▓▓▓	▓▓▓▓
Peach	Peach		
	Sweet Cherry Walnut		
	Morello Cherry - Berry Fruit		
		All Other Types of Fruit	
			Grape